Letters at Midnight

ROLAND B. KING

WordCrafts

Letters At Midnight
Copyright © 2013
Roland B. King

Cover Art Copyright © 2013 by Breanna King

All rights reserved. No part of this book may be reproduced, stored in a retrieval system, or transmitted in any form or by any means – electronic, mechanical, photocopy, recording, or otherwise – without the prior written permission of the publisher. The only exception is brief quotations for review purposes.

Published by WordCrafts Press
Tullahoma, TN 37388
www.wordcrafts.net

CONTENTS

◆◆◆

1	MOSES VS. SOLOMON
2	HELLO I'M BACK
3	THE EVENING AND THE MORNING
4	A CHAPTER WAY IN THE BACK?
5	WE WILL NOT ALL SLEEP BUT WE'LL ALL BE CHANGED
6	EVERY DAY IS LIKE SUNDAY
7	DENOMINATIONS, DENOMINATIONS, GET YOUR DENOMINATIONS!
8	IT IS EXPEDIENT THAT OFFENSES COME
9	MOSES VS. SOLOMON ROUND TWO
10	REVELATIONS
11	INSIGHTS
12	WHERE DID CAIN'S WIFE COME FROM?
13	YOU WERE A MAN BEFORE YOU BECAME A BOY
14	"THERE WILL BE NO WINE UNTIL IT'S TIME!" –JESUS
15	WE THOUGHT IT THE MOST BORING READING
16	AND HE LED THEM TO MARAH
17	BURNT STONES NEHEMIAH
18	NOTHING NEW UNDER THE SUN
19	WE'RE STILL NOT SATISFIED
20	HEART OF JERUSALEM
21	DÉJÀ VU
22	081689

23	LECTURES AT MIDNIGHT
24	"YEAH MOSES!" (WITH CLINCHED FISTS)
25	LETTERS AT MIDNIGHT
26	TWO KINDS OF PEOPLE
27	I DON'T LIKE THE CURRENT PRESIDENT
28	THE LORD IS GOD OF THE HILLS BUT HE IS NOT GOD OF THE VALLEYS
29	MOSES & THE PROMISED LAND
30	THE LAST SUPPER
31	NERO KESRON
32	THE DOMINANT CULTURE
33	EVANGELISM EXPLOSION

To the hand of Providence,
Who always pushes me away at first,
To see if I'm serious.

&

To our Lord Jesus Christ

Who in the midst of a hostile Dominant Culture
Had this to say concerning God's Truth:

"Look upon the fields. For they are ripe unto harvest."

His harvest.

1
MOSES VS. SOLOMON

Moses would not have been welcome in the Court of Solomon.

Or better said:

The Moses Dynamic, that fresh new move of God (which suddenly shows up in all its radicalness!), is never welcome in the Solomonic Moment.

—Those times when God has given his people rest.

And they are at peace with themselves and the Culture in which they live. Sound familiar?

Those wonderful church bells ringing every Sunday morning. I love them, but...

We who live in the Court of Solomon must not resist when a shabby prophet walks down our affluent corridors and says, *"I'm about to do a New Thing declares the Lord!"*

"A new thing?! Moses. Moses." – Solomon knows.

There is nothing new under the Sun.
Ecclesiastes 1:9

"And besides, change doesn't last."

For all the waters run into the sea yet the sea is never full.
Ecclesiastes 1:7

"But...
"Yet...
"Somehow..."
Up walks Moses.

Something from the absolute fringe of our mental society.
That thing too big to dream of!
That speck-of-hope never closer than the horizon.
For remember, Scripture says:

And Moses *drove* his cattle farther out than any other man.
Why?

Moses was looking for the edge.
Looking for the horizon.
Looking for the margin.
And Solomon will be the first to admit, "Kings don't write the stuff in the margin. That's extra reading. Material not really required. Added for deeper understanding. Kings and even Ex-Presidents write best-sellers."

So enters God...

Into our settled comfortable lives, saying, "There's more."
Whether it's more in worship.
More in devotion.
More in faith.
There's more.
(The life of Elijah proves there's more.)

"But he was special."
A man of like passions!
"Wait, that means he was just like us."

We who live in the Court of Solomon would do well to remember what James wrote: "When you see a different thing, an unfamiliar thing, *a new thing!* coming into your assembly, and not longing for change, your heart would give it a lesser seat, a back seat. Oh give it the chiefest seat, put it on the front pew of your heart!...'cause it just might be...the greatest move of God (in your life!) you've ever known."

And these are: **Letters At Midnight**.

2
HELLO I'M BACK

Tonight I'd like to talk of the misconception of strength. We know that nothing is put in the scriptures haphazardly. –For no reason at all. And yet the gospel writer Mark did just that.
Well...what appeared to be just that.
Okay I knew it wasn't that.
And it bothered me for years!
You know the instance I'm talking about. **Mark 14:48-53**. The young man who followed Jesus to the Garden the night of his betrayal. Yes, that guy. Who was he?

> *And Jesus answered and said unto the crowd, "Are you come out as against a thief, with swords and staves to take me? I was daily with you in the temple teaching, and you took me not, but the scriptures must be fulfilled."*
> *And they all forsook him and fled.*
> *And there followed him a certain young man having a linen cloth cast about his naked body and the young men laid hold on him and he left the linen cloth and fled from them naked.*

> *And they led Jesus away to the high priest and with him were assembled all the chief priests and the elders and the scribes.*

In the garden of Gethsemane this young man watched from a distance...was grabbed by the mob...lost his robe...his only piece of clothing?...and fled.
The end.
Never mentioned again.
Who?

This bothered me for years. Who was he? What was he doing there?

Jesus' disciples, the ones destined to become the Great Apostles, had already failed at any attempts to help.
Fled. Terrified. One showing back up later just to deny Him.
But here's this young man. Not called a disciple. Wearing only a robe. Grabbed. Then fleeing naked. Never, ever to be spoken of again.
I must admit. The vagueness of the event mused my curiosity to acute meditations.
Who was he!

Then one night. One blessed night. One "wonderfully awful" blessed night. —Yes, the Grinch was on my television screen with his feet frozen ice cold in the snow; and the silent stars were drifting by; O Little Town of Bethlehem was playing in the background also—suddenly it hit me.

Remember that angel that came down in the Gospel of Luke to strengthen Jesus when He was so sorrowful He was to the point of death, sweating as it were great drops of blood? That angel? The one who showed up to *STRENGTHEN THE LORD*. How do you strengthen the LORD?

> *And there appeared an angel unto Him from heaven, strengthening Him.*
> *And being in agony He prayed more earnestly and His sweat was as it were great drops of blood falling down to the ground.*
> **Luke 22:43,44**

Did you know it never mentions the angel departing? In fact he was with Jesus until the guards showed up and took Jesus away.

And then! Watched from a distance. Someone of the angry mod grabbed at him, caught him by his robe and the angel fled naked.

The angel in Mark 14, the one who showed up to strengthen the Lord, was not the typical 8-foot tall envisioned warrior-like being; but was in fact...an unassuming, harmless-looking young man.

Jesus, never forgetting the Spirit He was of, chose a mild mannered messenger instead of the powerful god-like warriors that will accompany Him at his second coming.

3
THE EVENING AND THE MORNING

This was performed before a packed house during Second Service at SA (Now Springhouse) March 3rd, 2002. Neither the church leadership, the congregation, nor I were prepared for the rush of God's Spirit that ensued:

"Good morning. First I'd like to thank Senior Pastors Ronnie and Wayne for encouraging the public display of the Gifts of the Spirit through the Arts.

"And second, I'd like to dedicate this to my wife who has befriended a 'possum that lives in the woods behind our house. It shows up on our back deck around midnight once a week and eats our cat's food, always knowing we're glad to see it.

"Scriptures teach that all Creation praises God. It's only mankind that's catching up. The ocean, sky, mountains, trees of the field, Winter, Spring, Summer and Fall all wait their turn to praise Him.

"But did you know...some of Creation...even has to

battle for their turn to praise?"
    Especially:

THE EVENING AND THE MORNING

DANCE!
DANCE!
DANCE!
THE FOREST IS AT WAR!
SO DANCE!!

THE WIND PLAYS SPOOKY TUNES GOING
    THROUGH THE TREES
JOGGING WEAKENED BRANCHES
BUMPING ENDLESSLY
WHISTLING SWIFTLY
ANOTHER RUSHING BREEZE!
THROWING!
TOSSING!
TEARING!
CHASING FRIGHTENED LEAVES
THE FOG ENCAMPS ITS MIST
HE THROWS HIS NET OF DEW
THE GRASS NOT ESCAPING
THE WATER TAKEN TOO
THE DARKENED AIR ADVANCES!!
THE DAY
IS SUDDENLY GONE
OUR BOWMAN BLEEDING THE WESTERN SKY
LIES ON AN ORANGE STREAKED LAWN
HE TRIES TO FIGHT BEING WEARY

IN DUSK HE SLIPS BENEATH
CONQUERED!
THE FOREST IS GIVEN UP
UNTO HIS TIMELY SLEEP

DANCE!
DANCE!
DANCE!
THE NIGHT HAS WON THE DAY!
SO DANCE!!

BLOW THE TREES OF EVERGREEN
TRIP THE TINY FERNS
WAKE THE WEEPING WILLOWS
TAKE NO PRISONER'S TERMS
SING FOREST!
REJOICE YOU DARKENED WOOD!
NIGHTTIME IS HERE AND PRAISING
SO BEWARE MY BLACKENED HOOD!
FRIENDS COME OUT COME JOIN ME
MAKE MERRY OUR TIME IS NOW...
—INSTANTLY SHADOWS APPEAR
—WIDE EYES OF HOOTING OWLS
—WRINKLED NOSES OF OPOSSUMS SNIFF THE
    PALPITATING AIR
—AS COUSINS (NOT NOCTURNAL)
—COUNT SILENT HEADS IN THREATENED LAIRS

TO THE REIGN OF THE PAPER TIGER
NIGHT'S CLAMOR!
RACKET!

ROAR!
THE UNFAMILIAR SOUND AT MIDNIGHT
A SUDDEN JIGGLE OF A LOCK AT A DOOR
A SUDDEN JIGGLE OF A LOCK AT A DOOR?

A FRIEND ENTREATING ENTRANCE?
AN ANGEL BEARING LIGHT?
IF IT'S YOUR TURN TO PRAISE GOD
'TIS A THIEF IN THE NIGHT!!

OUR BOWMAN IN YONDER EASTERN SKY FROM
    SETTING
QUICKLY WAKES!
A SPEAR APPEARS
A CRY!!! — IS HEARD
A SHADOW FALLS AND SHAKES
ARROWS FLY OF BRILLIANT COLOR
PIERCING NIGHTTIME'S SHIELD
THE FOG RETREATS...CAUTIOUSLY
FREEING THE CAPTURED FIELD

THE BLOCKADE BREAKS
THE FRONT IS TAKEN
THE HORIZON FALLING BELOW
SOPHISTICATION UPON HIS BROW AGAIN HE
    REARS HIS BOW

DARKNESS GRAYING
THE BATTLE WAGING
OUR BOWMAN HITS HIS MARK!
NIGHTTIME'S CLOAK DRIFTS FATALLY WOUNDED

LIGHT'S FULL SPECTRUM THROUGH THE HEART

THE FOREST HAS BEEN RESCUED
IS HEARD!
A CHEERING SIGH
TWO GALLOPING DOVES LEAP THE LAKE KISSING
    THE DEW GOOD-BYE

THE COUNTRYSIDE IS PASTEL
THERE BLOWS A GENTLE GALE
GRATEFUL FLOWERS
OPEN
TO
BLOOM
AND
MORNING
LIFTS
HER VEIL

NOW REVELING
WHILE YET CLIMBING
UPON GOD'S DOTTED LINE OF CHANCE?

THE SUN'S GOLDEN RAYS
LIKE A MILLION FEET

CONTINUES...

IN THE DANCE.

4
A CHAPTER WAY IN THE BACK?

Then Jesus departed into the coasts of Tyre and Sidon. And behold a woman of Canaan came out of the same coasts, and cried unto him, saying, Have mercy on me, O Lord, son of David: my daughter is grievously vexed with a devil.

But He answered her not a word. And his disciples came and besought him, saying, Send her away; for she crieth after us. But He answered and said, I am not sent but unto the lost sheep of the house of Israel.

Then came she and worshipped him, saying, Lord help me. But He answered and said, It is not meet to take the children's bread, and to cast it to dogs.

And she said, Truth, Lord: yet the dogs eat of the crumbs which fall from their master's table. Then Jesus answered and said unto her, O woman, great is thy faith: be it unto thee even as thou wilt. And her daughter was made whole from that very hour.

Matthew 15:21-28

A chapter way in the back?

But by now you should know where I'm going.
"Trust in meeee." —Unlike Kaa in the Jungle Book who sings that to the little boy Mowgli while his eyes are twirling, swirling whirlpools, hypnotizing the young lad. My eyes aren't whirlpools. They're blood shot. It's late. I should be sleeping but I've got to write. I must. These are **Letters At Midnight**.

So...
Tonight I want to applaud the times that God has gone out of his way to offend me.
Say it with me: "Offend me."
Ah, you say that as if there have been times He's offended you.
"You mean my offenses aren't unique! But like things happen to all of us."
(As the scriptures teach.)

Then let's applaud the heroes of offenses mentioned in the Bible:
The first one that comes to mind is Elisha in **II Kings 2**.

> *And it came to pass when the Lord would take up Elijah into heaven by a whirlwind... that Elijah said unto Elisha,* ***WAIT HERE FOR THE LORD HAS SENT ONLY ME TO BETHEL.***
> *And Elisha said,* ***AS THE LORD LIVETH***

AND AS YOUR SOUL LIVETH I WILL NOT LEAVE YOU.

And they went on to Bethel.

And the sons of the prophets who lived at Bethel came out and said to Elisha, ***YOU DO KNOW THAT THE LORD WILL TAKE YOUR MASTER FROM YOU TODAY, DON'T YOU?***

And Elisha Said, ***I KNOW IT. BE QUIET!***

And Elijah said to Elisha, ***ELISHA, WAIT HERE FOR THE LORD HAS SENT ONLY ME TO JERICHO.***

And Elisha said, ***AS THE LORD LIVETH AND AS YOUR SOUL LIVETH I WILL NOT LEAVE YOU.***

And they went to Jericho.

And the sons of the prophets who lived at Jericho came out and said to Elisha, ***YOU DO KNOW THAT THE LORD WILL TAKE YOUR MASTER FROM YOU TODAY, DON'T YOU?***

And Elisha said, ***I KNOW IT. BE QUIET!***

And Elijah said unto Elisha, ***WAIT HERE, THIS TIME WAIT HERE, FOR THE LORD HAS SENT ONLY ME TO JORDAN.***

And Elisha said, ***AS THE LORD LIVETH AND AS YOUR SOUL LIVETH I WILL NOT LEAVE YOU.***

And the two left together.

And as they stood by the Jordan
...the sons of the prophets afar off
...Elijah smote the waters and the two went

over on dry land.
Then Elijah said to Elisha, **NOW ASK WHAT YOU WANT BEFORE I AM TAKEN UP FROM YOU THAT YOU MAY HAVE IT.**
And Elisha said, **LET A DOUBLE PORTION OF THY SPIRIT BE UPON ME.**
And Elijah thought, **WOW!**

"Get it Charlie Brown? Isn't it great!"
(I can't help it, I've had three little children and after seeing the same cartoons a thousand times they're stuck in my head forever.)
But you do realize what the story is actually saying?
"Charlie?"

TRANSLATION:
Elijah was on his way (wherever that was—you see he didn't know, God was even offending him) walking from place to place waiting on whenever God decided to show up with the Horseman of Israel and cart him away on a fiery chariot and Elisha *his disciple wouldn't stop following.*
"Man you're buggin me," Elijah says to him in verse 2. Elijah goes to the next place. Elisha follows.
"Cut it out! I want to be alone. Besides, the Lord has only sent me to these places. He hasn't said anything about you. He doesn't even know you're with me." The great prophet complains in verses 4 and 6.
But Elisha *not only didn't* cut it out (a glorious

double negative, 'cause it's a chapter of offenses) but Elisha even said, "Don't try and discourage me, in fact I want a carbon copy, no wait, even twice the power you have!"

...And Elijah thought, "Wow! This guy's serious."

He wasn't offended. It was just a test.

"Do you really want what I've got Elisha?" Elijah was saying, "then prepare yourself for offenses."

And did Elisha get what he wanted?

> *And he took the mantle that fell from Elijah and smote the waters and said, "Where is the God of Elijah!" and when he had smitten the waters they parted. And Elisha went over on dry ground.*
>
> **II Kings 2:14**

The rest is Hero history.

Then there's Jesus, the Bread of Life crying to his new, I mean *new*, followers:

"Unless you eat my flesh and drink my blood you won't live!"

Being familiar with the Levitical law and its prohibition on cannibalism they were horrifically offended.

It was just a test.

Jesus later saying, "I was merely spiritually speaking."

But my favorite? It's **Matthew 15**, when Jesus

took the prejudice of his day and not only disarmed it but empowered the object of the prejudice. That's right, when He called the Syrophoenician woman a dog. *A dog.* To say He didn't call her that and make him so-called politically correct would be an injustice to her. He called her *what the culture of that day* considered her and then elevated her and her faith to a place of honor few aspire to.

"Oh woman," He said, "Your faith is great."

(Like Abraham's, Isaac's, Jacob's, David's, all the hall-of-famers in **Hebrews 11**.)

"Even the dogs eat the crumbs from their master's tables, Lord," she said. She wasn't offended.

Great was her faith.

Great was His compassion.

Mighty was his power.

Healed was her daughter.

And destroyed was the prejudice of the day.

Praise God.

Let's applaud the offenses of God that come our way. They're only a test. His love is sure.

Let us be people of courage.

Disciples of understanding.

Grateful children.

And recipients...of the blessing to follow.

P.S. Now read the first line of this chapter again:

Then Jesus departed INTO THE COASTS OF TYRE AND SIDON, and behold a woman of

Canaan came out OF THE SAME COASTS, and cried unto him, saying, "Have mercy on me, O Lord, son of David: my daughter is GRIEVOUSLY VEXED WITH A DEVIL."

JESUS MADE A SPECIAL TRIP down to a *Gentile* coastal town because there (His Heavenly Father had told him) a desperate mother lived with a daughter so afflicted they could have never traveled to him.

For this purpose the Son of God was manifested, that He might destroy all the works of the devil.

1 John 3:8

JESUS WENT ALL THIS WAY ALL THIS TIME *JUST TO HELP HER.*
Puts a different twist on it, doesn't it.

When God is pushing us away with one hand, His heart is reaching out with the other.
But He's looking for something in us.
Maybe a certain reaction.
And it's always…
FAITH.

5
WE WILL NOT ALL SLEEP BUT WE'LL ALL BE CHANGED

"Will we know each other in the Resurrection?" Yes. Be sure of it.

> *And I say unto you, that many shall come from the east and west and shall sit down with Abraham, Isaac, and Jacob in the kingdom of Heaven.*
> **Matthew 8:11**

We'll know people we even didn't know.
In fact the only time we won't know each other is when we deliberately hide our identity. Like Jesus did on the road to Emmaus.

"I'll finally see Maw-maw again."
"And meet my other grandmother for the first time."
"O, glorious."

"What will we be like?"

Jesus, when appearing to his frightened disciples after his resurrection, said:

Touch me, for a spirit has not flesh and bone.

Paul said:

I show you a mystery: flesh and blood cannot inherit the kingdom of God.

Get it? Isn't it amazing?

The only thing that will be different is... we'll have no blood.

We'll have flesh and bone Jesus said.

But we won't have blood Paul wrote.

In fact we'll be able to walk through walls or suddenly appear like Jesus did; and then be able to be hugged and eat fish like Jesus did too.

"Sounds like a glorified body to me."

"Did He not say we'd eat with Him at the marriage supper of the Lamb!"

"But we'll have no blood."

Scriptures say the life is in the blood.
And so are diseases.
And it's why we get tired.
And over there we'll never sleep.

"And we'll live."
"We live!"

By the blood of Christ.
The glorious wonderful life giving blood of Christ.

6
EVERY DAY IS LIKE SUNDAY

"...Everyday is silent and [grey]." (English spelling.)

Because it's English. And only a line out of one of my all time favorite songs. We all have them; let's not hide.

When I first became a Christian every Sunday the message was tailor made for me.

The Lord read my mail, or even better, wrote mail to me every Sunday. As the years passed by, Sundays became silent and grey.

Then filled again with enthusiasm!

Then again, times of fall.

Silent and grey.

But one thing stays the same. The Lord never lets me forsake his house. No matter what my state of mind or my level of receiving from Him.

Naomi the mother-in-law of Ruth in the lineage of Jesus lost her husband and sons after she left the house of bread and praise.

> Now it came to pass in the days when the judges ruled, that there was a famine in the land. And a certain man of Bethlehem-Judah went out to sojourn in the country of Moab, he and his wife and his two sons.
> And the name of the man was Elimelech and the name of his wife Naomi, and the name of his two sons Mahlon and Chilion, Ephrathites of Bethlehem-Judah. And they came into the country of Moab, and continued there.
> And Elimelech Naomi's husband died and she was left and her two sons.
> And they took them wives of the women of Moab, the name of the one Orpah, and the name of the other Ruth: and they dwelled there about ten years.
> And Mahlon and Chilion died also both of them; and the woman was left of her two sons and her husband.
> Then she arose with her daughters-in-law, that she might return from the country of Moab; for she had heard in the country of Moab how that **THE LORD HAD VISITED HIS PEOPLE GIVING THEM BREAD**.

"Gee." To lose your spouse and both children in one decade.

They left Bethlehem-Judah because of the famine

in their lives.

God would caution, "don't leave Bethlehem-Judah." Which means house of bread and praise. "Suddenly the Lord (whom you seek) will appear in his temple." The scriptures speak of Jesus when He was just twelve, a child, suddenly appearing in his temple and amazing everyone.

God is saying, "even if you're sitting numb on a pew at a church, one morning Jesus will show up for you, and your life in Christ will be like you're a child again." You'll be amazed.

>   Trust me.
>   That's what He's saying.
>   That's what He's telling you.
>   He's again reading your mail.
>   And it's all good.

7
DENOMINATIONS, DENOMINATIONS, GET YOUR DENOMINATIONS!

Isn't it wonderful. All the denominations in the body of Christ.
"What?"
Yes.

God's in control. Do we think we wouldn't look this way unless He wanted us to?
We're His church, a kingdom that transcends all boundaries.
If it was as simple as a nation, He'd have states, or provinces run by governors and mayors. In the Old Testament it was Israel, divided into 12 tribes, with elders and heads of family lines. But being a church, He's ordained denominations with pastors and teachers, evangelists, etc. How did we think He was going to do it?
A Kingdom *has to be put some way* into manageable parts. And since it's no longer

geographical or hereditary, it's denominational.

When Jesus fed the multitudes He made them sit down in groups of fifty and hundreds.

"That's odd."

"Just feed them."

"Why put them in groups?"

Because He still gives us our daily bread and He still puts us in groups.

I Corinthians 12:18 says:
He sets all the members in the body as He sees fit.

He still puts us in groups.

"Yet sadly...

"One of the worst?...

"Occurrences in the whole of the Bible...

"Is recorded in **Judges 12:5,6**

"...And how it goes quietly unnoticed."

And the Gileadites took the passages of Jordan before the Ephraimites. And it was so that when the Ephraimites which were escaped said, "Let me pass," that the men of Gilead said unto them.

"Are you an Ephraimite?"

And if he said, "No,"

Then they said, "Then say the word, shibboleth."

> *And he said 'Sibboleth' for he could not frame to pronounce it right. Then they took him and slew him!*
>
> *And at the passages of Jordan there fell at that time of Ephraimites 42,000.*

How terrible.

Two tribes, brothers of Israel, killing each other because they didn't say *the same Word the same way.*

"And they shall know you are my people by the love you have for one another."

Jesus said that. He has the better way. Love. But He still puts us in *different* groups.

Find a church. One that speaks to you. And grow in the knowledge and grace of Christ. Give of your precious time.

And get more than you ever thought possible.

8
IT IS EXPEDIENT THAT OFFENSES COME

Currently the state in which I live is in the process of adopting a state lottery.

The funding of education will be helped by the lottery.
And so will the pawn shop industry.
This last election I of course voted my conscience.
—My children may still be reading from old books.
—But I won't be pawning their new ones either.

Regardless of my position on the matter, the fact is things will take place that will affect society, positively or adversely, that we have no power of stopping. I repeat, even though we are the people of God whose prayers affect the Heavens, there are some things that happen in our culture that are out of our control, even our prayers.
Jesus said, it is expedient (necessary, ordained) that some offenses come.
The important thing is...where do we stand or kneel when these offenses happen?

In the book of Ezekiel when the glory of God is visiting the Earth and He sees all the abominations done in the temple and He's sending the Babylonians for the last time to finish the job of destroying His defiled dwelling place; He calls for an angel that is holding an inkhorn. This angel is to go about the city before the last assault and mark the foreheads of all the people who grieve over the wickedness done in the city. They were the only ones to be spared alive in the attack:

> *And he cried also in my ears with a loud voice, saying, Cause them that have charge over the city to draw near, even every man with his destroying weapon in his hand.*
> *And behold six men came from the way of the higher gate, which lies toward the north, and every man a slaughter weapon in his hand; and one man among them was clothed with linen, with a writer's inkhorn by his side: and they went in, and stood beside the brazen altar.*
> *And the glory of the God of Israel was gone up from the cherub, whereupon he was, to the threshold of the house. And he called to the man clothed with linen, which had the writer's inkhorn by his side;*
> *And the LORD said unto him, Go through the midst of the city, through the midst of Jerusalem, and set a mark upon the foreheads of the men that sigh and that cry for all the*

abominations that be done in the midst thereof.

And to the others he said in my hearing, Go ye after him through the city, and smite; let not your eye spare, neither have you pity:

Slay utterly old and young, both maids and little children and women; but come not near any one upon whom is the mark; and begin at my sanctuary.

Then they began...

Ezekiel 9:1-6

Understand?

These people, who *had no power whatsoever* to change the negative things in their society, were spared alive because of the fact that *at least they grieved* over the wickedness being done.

As we leave the Solomonic moment where society once embraced Christian ideals and enter into the Moses dynamic where we stand in opposition to the dominant culture, whether we individually succeed or not, God notices us because we at least grieve for the death and decay of our land.

Letters At Midnight. I never said they'd be easy.

9
MOSES VS SOLOMON ROUND TWO

There are Two...
Great...
Irreconcilable!...
Godly...

Opposing Forces operating in a person's life.

And if the individual could ever harness these together.
"Have them work in unity."
Well to put it in the words of Elijah as he rode the chariot to Heaven, "The sky's the limit!"
They are: **CHANGE** and **COMFORT**.

Change in a person's life is depicted in the narrative of Moses. In fact, the people of Moses' day saw the greatest of change in their lives. Their whole Culture (i.e. world) collapsing around them. God bringing the individual into a New Reality. A New Freedom.

Then there's Solomon. Who represents those Comfort-zones God intends for us to have. It was Solomon who reigned during the Golden Age of Israel. Israel's only Golden Age.
Those long periods of rest in a person's life.
When God is establishing the individual.
Promoting. Securing. Blessing the person. Giving us comfort-zones:

So Judah and Israel lived in safety every man under his vine and fig tree all the days of Solomon.
1 Kings 4:25

Solomon *then pondering* (like you and I are supposed to be) *from a state of rest,*
The change that must come:

TO EVERY THING THERE IS A SEASON! AND A TIME TO EVERY PURPOSE UNDER HEAVEN.
(*Turn Turn Turn.* The Band. The Birds. Whatever.)

So...
There are in every person's life, working at all times at some level of intensity, these two Godly Opposing forces:
Moses and Solomon. Change and Comfort.

And Scripture teaches...if we could ever harness these two...
"Yoke them together?"

"Have them working in the same direction in our lives?"
"Accept them with the same favor from the Lord?'"
"Change and Comfort?"
"Moses and Solomon?!"

Scripture declares:

Where brethren walk together
In unity (It's THERE!)
The oil (The Holy Spirit!)
Flows down Aaron's beard (Jesus! Our High Priest.)
Psalm 133

—And the anointing of God enters our life.
—And we're empowered to do the things He's called us to do.
—Operate in the giftings He's gifted us with.
—And love the lost with the Love of Christ, the way only the Spirit can.
So embrace Change.
Embrace Comfort.
And find yourself—
Embracing Christ.

Letters At Midnight.
"And I saw it was a time for a change."
First I quote the Birds now the Stones?

10
REVELATIONS

The Book of Revelations is about dilemmas. The devil is in dilemma with God. The church is in dilemma with Christ. The Christian and the world can no longer live together. The nations are angry. And the old creation senses a new one coming.

But.

The greatest dilemma in the book of Revelations is the dilemma God had...

WITH HIMSELF.

Revelation 5 says that before the foundation of the world, when God wrote History, God wrote all the names of the people He loved in a book. The Book of Life. And these people in this book, He wanted them to experience a second life. An eternal life. A resurrection. So that they would be with Him and enjoy Him forever.

But!

He also knew that the people represented by the names in this book would become sinful and He'd have to seal the book with seven deadly seals that contained the fullness of God's wrath. So God had a dilemma. The love He wanted to show sealed by His wrath because of our sins.

GOD'S LOVE SEALED BY GOD'S WRATH.

And He also knew, the only way to solve this dilemma was for the Godhead to do it Himself. So the Son became flesh and dwelt among us and we beheld His glory as the only begotten of the Father full of grace and truth. And He offered Himself up by the Holy Spirit.

And the Son purchased this book, the Book of Life, with His own blood. That's why it's called the Lamb's Book of Life. He purchased every name in the book. And that's why Paul wrote,

Therefore if any man be in Christ Jesus he is a new creature old things are passed away (our sin, God's wrath, the seals) *and behold all things* are/can/and will/the Resurrection *become new*, take place.

Because of Christ.

This is:

REVELATIONS

I JOHN WAS IMPRISONED ON THE ISLE OF PATMOS FOR THE TESTIMONY OF GOD. AND BEING IN THE SPIRIT ON THE LORD'S DAY, YES, REJOICING IN MY CHAINS; SUDDENLY I HEARD A VOICE BEHIND ME SAYING, "COME HERE. I WANT TO SHOW YOU SOMETHING" AND TURNING I SAW...

IN THE HAND OF HIM WHO SAT ON THE THRONE
    A BOOK!
WHOSE CONTENTS I COULD ONLY WONDER
ASSURED THE SEVEN SEALS THAT BOUND IT!
CLAMORED THE CLANKING THUNDER!

THE BOOK OF LIFE WHICH BORE OUR NAMES
    BOUND SHUT?
BY THE FULLNESS OF GOD'S WRATH?
WHO IS WORTHY TO OPEN THE BOOK?!
LOUDLY THE LIGHTNING LAUGHED!

THEN HOW SHALL THE MEEK INHERIT THE
    EARTH
WHEN GOD JUDGES THE WORLD FOR SIN?
FOR ALL HAVE SINNED FALLING SHORT OF HIS
    GLORY!
...EVEN THE NAMES OF HIS FRIENDS

THE BOOK OF LIFE BOUND SHUT
BY SEVEN DEADLY SEALS
CRYING HOLY! HOLY! HOLY! OBLIVIOUS!
TO HOW I FEEL!

I BEGAN TO WEEP
FOR WHO COULD THERE EVER BE
WHILE JUDGING THE UNRIGHTOUSNESS OF ALL
    MANKIND
MAKE A CLEFT IN THE ROCK FOR ME

I SAID I BEGAN TO WEEP!

—BUT ALL MY SUDDEN SINCERE TEARS
WERE DROWNED BY THE SOUND OF MANY WATERS
TORRENTS I'D MADE
FROM ALL MY SINFUL YEARS

WEEP NOT
A VOICE SAID
THE LION OF JUDAH PREVAILED

QUICKLY I LOOKED
AND IN THE MIDST OF THE ELDERS AND FOUR BEASTS
A LITTLE LAMB LAY SLAIN
HIS PAWS PIERCED WITH NAILS

HE IS WORTHY TO OPEN THE BOOK
TO LOOSE THE SEALS THEREOF
FOR WHO MORE WORTHY TO SHOW GOD'S WRATH
THEN HE WHO SHOWED ONLY LOVE

AND THE LAMB WAS CAUGHT UP TO THE THRONE
THE HIGHEST THRONE!
WHERE GOD HAD PREPARED HIM A PLACE
ADORED BY ALL THE ANGELS
CHERUBS, SERAPHIM BEHOLDING HIS REGAL FACE

"THY THRONE O GOD! IS FOREVER"

THE FATHER SWEARING PROCLAIMED
"LET EVERY THING THAT HAS BREATH," THE SPIRIT SPOKE
"WORSHIP JESUS' NAME."

BUT THERE WAS SILENCE IN HEAVEN

AS THE LAMB WITHOUT SIN WHO NOW SAT ON THE THRONE
CRACKED! THE FIRST SEAL ON THE BOOK OF LIFE
AND JESUS CAST THE FIRST STONE!

WAR BROKE OUT!
THE DEVIL AND HIS ANGELS FOUGHT!
—BUT THERE WAS NO PLACE FOR THEM
THE SON RULED THE NATIONS WITH AN IRON ROD
AND LIKE CLAY POTS ON A SHELF DASHED AT THE SLIGHTEST WHIM

AND GREAT SIGNS APPEARED
AS TRUMPETS BEGAN TO SOUND!
HEAVEN AND EARTH FLEEING AWAY!
BUT AGAIN NO PLACE WAS FOUND

AND THE ONE SCRIPTURE CALLS THE SON OF MAN
WHO WALKED AS A SERVANT TWO THOUSAND YEARS AGO

CHARGED BY ON A STALLION, HIS VESTURE IN

BLOOD!
HIS RAIMENT WHITE AS SNOW!
SO HIGH AND LIFTED UP
HIS ROBE THE ROLLING CLOUDS!
FOLLOWED BY ALL THE ARMIES OF HEAVEN
AND TEN THOUSAND CHEERING CROWDS!

AND HE CAUSED THE MEEK TO INHERIT ALL THE LANDS
AND AS GOD'S FOOT TOUCHED THE EARTH
CREATION WHO'D BEEN WAITING
ON THE MANIFESTATION OF THE CHILDREN OF GOD
EXPEREINCED...A REBIRTH.

Performed Advent 2004

11
INSIGHTS

You know these are just thoughts.

Insights I've received through the years.
Some 25 years old. Some since yesterday.
'Cause I'm:

Like a householder bringing forth old and new things out of my storehouse.
Matthew 13:52

But of course you know that's what He meant.
"Actually I think the Word of God is like a Rock, and I haven't even scratched the surface yet."
(Me too! But hold that thought. We'll devote a whole letter to that later.)

SO, WHAT ABOUT THE PARABLE OF THE SOWER OF THE SEED?

You know, the one where the sower went out to sow and he threw the Word of God on four types of soil and only one brought forth lasting fruit.

25%

Wow. If you're a child in school that's a failing grade.
But if you're a grown man and an investor, that's great!

What's the interest on your house mortgage? If your lending institution could get 25% on your loan I think they'd be ecstatic, although you might not be too happy about it.

25% success rate on the randomly thrown word of God.
A failing grade as a child. Gargantuan as a man.
Share the Word. It has a very high success rate.
And remember:
THE POWER'S IN THE MESSAGE NOT THE MESSENGER.

A sower went out to sow…and simply tossed seed.
P.S. —The same place you tossed seed one day may have been plowed on another, now readied as good soil for the Word of God. Don't give up.
A sower went out to sow…and simply tossed seed.

Goodnight, it's past Twelve. And these are **Letters At Midnight**.

12
WHERE DID CAIN'S WIFE COME FROM?

Have I mentioned the shortest chapters in the history of human literature?
Well...

I'm back! Today at work I heard a co-worker remark how Cain, after murdering his brother Abel (how terrible), went out to the land of Nod and found a wife. And that if you want to find a wife just nod at what they say and you'll get one.
A bad joke? I would probably be having carry-out for dinner; but since it was done in my hearing I felt obliged to address the issue.
To many, this is one of the greatest inconsistencies of the Bible. (Again, how terrible.) But this story is one of the most perceived fallacies of all Scripture:

> *And Adam knew Eve his wife and she conceived and bare Cain, and said, I have*

gotten a man from the Lord.

And she again bare his brother Abel. And Abel was a keeper of sheep, but Cain was a tiller of the ground.

AND IN PROCESS OF TIME *(there's the key) it came to pass, that Cain brought of the fruit of the ground an offering unto the lord.*

And Abel, he also brought of the firstlings of his flock and of the fat thereof. And the Lord had respect unto Abel and to his offering.

But unto Cain and to His offering the Lord had not respect. And Cain was very wroth and his countenance fell.

...And Cain talked with Abel his brother; AND IT CAME TO PASS, when they were in the field, that Cain rose up against his brother and slew him.

...AND CAIN WENT OUT FROM THE PRESENCE OF THE LORD, AND DWELT IN THE LAND OF NOD, ON THE EAST OF EDEN.

And Cain knew his wife and she conceived...

Genesis 4:4,5,8,16-17

"Okay. Where really did Cain's wife come from?"
"If Adam and Eve gave birth to Cain and Abel..."
"And Cain murdered Abel and then left..."
"Where did his wife and the entire land of Nod come from?"

The answer? —Only the complete opposite of our Modern Contemporary Pre-conceived Perceptions.

"Huh?"
"What?"
Yes. — My fellow employees were questioning.

We live extremely short lives. Seventy years the Scriptures declare in **Psalm 90:10**. Then no guarantee of good heath, and even then seventy's old. I'm sorry Mom.

So we assume when Cain murdered Abel they were both young men. Well...they were, but not by our standards. The Bible says that they lived to just under a thousand years in those days.

Remember, "In the *day* you eat of the fruit you'll die," the LORD said.

"And *a thousand years is as one day* with the Lord," the New Testament records.

That's why no one ever lived to be a thousand. They died *that day*. Which was a *thousand-year day*. Methuselah who lived to be 969, the oldest man ever, can attest to that.

So we assume looking at the murder of Abel through the grid of our contemporary life spans that it happened earlier in both of their lives. When in actuality it happened much later. The murder of Abel happened right around when Adam was 130 years old.

> *And Adam **LIVED AN HUNDRED AND THIRTY YEARS, AND BEGAT A SON** in his own likeness, after his image; and called his name **SETH**.*

Genesis 5:3

*And Adam knew his wife again; and she bare a son; and called his name **SETH** (which means substitute, replacement); **FOR GOD SAID SHE, HATH APPOINTED ME ANOTHER SEED INSTEAD OF ABEL WHOM CAIN SLEW**.*
Genesis 4:25

She being 130 years old of just under a thousand year life span would have had more sons than just two; and here she reasons that God gave her another son whom Cain her oldest son had *just slew*. It was her first son after the death of Abel. His murder was fresh on her mind. And if a thousand years is as one day with our Heavenly Father, then his Son's murder is still very fresh on his mind. In fact in God's eyes it's just barely been two days. And Peter writes in **II Peter 3:3-4**:

*...There shall come in the last days scoffers walking after their own lusts saying, **WHERE IS THE PROMISE OF HIS COMING**?*

In fact, in 3:8 of the same chapter is the famous verse of the thousand years time clock with God. Trust me, Jesus' blood is still fresh on the mind of our Heavenly Father. He's still quite impassioned over what happened at the Cross.

But getting back to what a 130 year-old married couple would have been like back then. You're still driving the car home as fast as you can—'I'm sorry it's late.' But cousins, second cousins, third cousins, whole cities, were out there in the first 130 years of human existence. That's why the long life span; God kept them young even in their hundreds of years.

And God blessed them (Adam and Eve) *and God said unto them, be fruitful and multiply, and replenish the earth.*
Genesis 1:28

Replenish the Earth? Was it plenished before? Were Adam and Eve just the new tenants? (Possibly another letter?)

Cain murdered Abel. —Fled to the land of Nod, and found a wife.

P.S. We also assume that was the first murder. Probably, or most definitely, not. Scripture sees no problem at all with only highlighting the notable acts.
Adam and Eve were the first Christian family. And one of their sons murdered his brother. Kind of accentuates the story, now doesn't it.

P.S.S. How can Adam and Eve be the first Christian family? They were ancient Old Testament history.

And the **WORLD WAS MADE BY HIM** (Christ) *and the world knew him not.*

John 1

Yes, Christ was there.
At the beginning.
At the first.
And Creation was singing His praises then too:

"Where were you when I laid the foundation of the earth. Tell me, if you have understanding. Who set its measurements, since you know.

"Or who stretched the line on it? On what were its bases sunk? Who laid its cornerstone? When all the morning stars sang together.

"And all the sons of God shouted for joy?"
Job 38:4-7.

And if you can receive it, He was the One walking with Adam in the garden. (Shh...it's so late.)

13
You Were A Man Before You Became A Boy

Y OU WE'RE A MAN!

                                              John 1:10

BEFORE
YOU BECAME A BOY

                                              Luke 2:7

THE UNIVERSE WAS YOUR TOY

                                              John 1:3

THEN YOU RAN
WITH YOUR FRIENDS
IN THE DESERT SUN
YOU'D CLOSE YOUR EYES
AND IN THE BLACKNESS REMEMBER WHEN IT ALL
    BEGUN
BACK WHEN...

                                              Genesis 1:1-3

A CARPENTER'S KID

                              Matthew 13:55
WERE YOU ILLITERATE?
THE WORD MADE FLESH AND SPIRIT?
                              John 1:14

OHHHHHHH
THEY STOOD AMAZED
                              Luke 4:20

AS YOU READ WITH SUCH GRACE
                              Luke 4:22

"WHOSE CHILD IS THIS?" THEY WISHED
                              John 7:15

AS MOTHER MARY GAVE YOU A KISS
AND THEN THEY LEFT, YOU STAYED
                              John 7:10a

YOU WE'RE ALONE

BUT THEN!
SHOWED UP AT THE PARTY LATE
                              John 7:10b

SAYING THINGS
                              John 7:15

SO AHEAD OF YOUR DAYS
                              John 7:26

AND THEY SAID!...

EVEN WHEN THIS BOY'S LATE!
THE SON OF GOD
IS AHEAD OF HIS DAYS!
                              John 7:39

OHHHHHHH
EVEN WHEN THIS BOY'S LATE
THE SON OF GOD
IS AHEAD OF HIS DAYS

AND NOW
THERE IS SOMETHING HE WANTS US TO KNOW
THERE IS SOMETHING
HE WANTS US TO KNOW

John 16:12

THE UNIVERSE
MAY WAX VERY OLD

Hebrews 1:10,11

THIS NATION OF OURS
MAY SOMEDAY COME AND GO
YOU AND I
OUR LIVES
ARE LIKE A FOG ON THE ROAD

James 4:14

BUT THERE IS SOMETHING HE WANTS US TO KNOW
THERE IS SOMETHING
HE WANTS US TO KNOW

THE UNIVERSE
WILL WAX VERY OLD

THIS NATION OF OURS
WILL COME AND GO

YOU AND I
ARE ONLY TRAVELERS ON A ROAD

BUT THERE IS SOMETHING HE WANTS US TO KNOW
THERE IS SOMETHING
HE WANTS US TO KNOW

AND IT'S THIS: WE THINK HE'S GONNA SHOW UP NOW

BUT EVEN IF HE SHOWS UP LATE

2 Peter 3:9

THE SON OF GOD
IS AHEAD OF HIS DAYS

OHHHHHHH!

EVEN IF HE SHOWS UP LATE
THE SON OF GOD
IS STILL AHEAD OF HIS DAYS

ALWAYS AHEAD OF HIS DAYS
THE SON OF GOD
IS ALWAYS AHEAD OF HIS DAYS.

Revelation 22:13

14
"THERE WILL BE NO WINE UNTIL IT'S TIME!"
—JESUS

"Finally you said something that meant something to me."

This is what the employee back in Chapter 12 said after sharing my views. Okay, he just gave me a look. But that's what his look meant! I'm sure of it.

I'm sure...as I walked away shrugging my head also.

But hey, in this life we're all entitled to our own opinions.

Which reminds me of something. Isn't it curious the only ones that knew Jesus had turned the water into wine at the wedding feast of Cana were the servants and the disciples. The ones whose opinions meant nothing. In fact the ones who couldn't even share their opinions. Servants and disciples. Listen:

> *There was a wedding in Cana of Galilee and the mother of Jesus was there. And Jesus also was invited and His disciples to the wedding.*
>
> *And when the wine ran out the mother of Jesus said to him,* "**THEY HAVE NO WINE.**"
>
> *And Jesus said to her,* "**WOMAN WHAT HAVE I TO DO WITH YOU, MY HOUR HAS NOT YET COME.**"
>
> *His mother said to the servants,* "**WHATEVER HE SAYS TO YOU, DO IT.**"
>
> *Now there were six stone water pots there containing thirty gallons each! And Jesus said,* "**FILL THEM TO THE BRIM.**"
>
> *And when the host had tasted the water that had become wine and did not know where it came from, but the servants who had drawn the water knew.*
>
> *The host said to the bridegroom,* "**YOU HAVE KEPT THE GOOD WINE UNTIL NOW!**"
>
> ***THIS BEGINNING OF MIRACLES DID JESUS IN CANA OF GALILEE, AND MANIFESTED HIS GLORY, AND HIS DISCIPLES BELIEVED ON HIM.***
>
> **John 2:1-11**

Do we know what's going on? Oh sinister! But understandably human.

The narrative lists Mary first. She's the main one invited in their group. Jesus and his disciples are mentioned second; they're secondary guests. Jesus hadn't done any miracles yet; He was merely her oldest son there with a bunch of his friends.

This part of the story is about Mary. All about Mary!

The wine had run out. Mary seeing the problem went to Jesus to correct it. Problem for Mary? It wasn't Mary's problem to fix; she was just a guest.

She says, "Jesus they have no wine."

He replies, "Woman what have I to do with you my hour has not yet come."

She's thinking, "I know son, but my hour has."

So picture it. Here is the mother Mary, after all the years of speculation of pre-marital promiscuity finally having the chance of saying, "Look at what Jesus did. See, He is the Son of God, I didn't conceive him illegitimately."

The only ones that knew of His great miracle of turning the water into wine were the servants whose opinions couldn't be spoken and the disciples who saw what Jesus had done but whose opinions were developing under the direction of their Master.

Voices unheard who kept silent of the whole matter.

Mary went on un-vindicated.

Jesus didn't care if they knew.

And the guests drank the best wine they'd ever had.

But!...
But...

Wait...
Just wait.
In Eternity when everything is shouted from the roof tops:
Mary is absolutely vindicated.
Jesus not only cares but dries every single tear.
And the wedding guests?...

Some long for just one of the days of the Son of Man.
Luke 17:22
And others are still at the party.
Matthew 22:1-10
Revelation 19:9

P.S. - Jesus didn't care if anyone knew of the miracle. His hour appointed by the Father had not yet come. The Son loves the Father and *only wants to please Him*. I'm in tears now comparing Jesus' devotion to the Father with mine. And Max, you're right, that's why they call Him the Savior—but that's over a dozen best-sellers ago.

P.S.S.

"What, another one?!"
"Can't you just finish a chapter without p.s.'s?"
"Does our law judge a man before it hears what he has to say?"
Hey, Nicodemus said that, but I can't put anything by you.

So P.S.S. — I've always found it curious that after Jesus says to Mary, "Woman what have I to do with you. My hour has not yet come."

That Mary's response was, "Whatever He tells you to do, do it."

She wasn't rebuffed by Jesus' reply at all. In fact! His reply *or the way he said it,* was actually leaning towards "*Yes, I'll help you,*" although his words clearly said, "*No, I won't.*"

He didn't answer her begrudgingly, "My time has not yet come."

He didn't answer her sternly, "Woman what have I to do with you?"

Well, being involved in acting circles, saying those kinds of words and having Mary perceive them as a Y*es* leans towards a humorous inflection.

"Son, they have no wine."

"There will be no wine until it's time!" an outraged Jesus jesters. (That's what his words meant.)

Mary smiling while turning to the servants, "What ever He says to do, do it. Trust me on this one. I know my boy."

It was a wedding. God was in a jovial mood.

We don't think God knows how to be in a jovial mood at a wedding? In scripture the two most joyous occasions are a wedding and...

The birth of a child.

Oww! Another **Letter At Midnight**?

15
WE THOUGHT IT THE MOST BORING READING

And thou shall make the Tabernacle after the pattern that was shown thee in the Mount.
Exodus 26:30

"Make sure thou makest it exactly to the pattern."
"Don't deviate an inch Moses!"
"Make it a perfect copy Moses."
"Don't even..."
"Dot every..."
"Cross every..."
"Moses!"
"Moses!"
"Moses!"

Remember he was the lawgiver. And that requires 100 percent perfection.

For if you fail in one point you're guilty of all.
James 2:10

"Yeah Moses!"
"Make it after every thing that was shown thee in the Mount."
"Moses."

Poor Moses. The curtain, the poles, the altar, the...
Everything! A complete exact replica of the heavenly vision.
Poor Moses trying to copy that.

But did you know...
Did you know...
Do you know...

There is one and only one object God didn't set measurements for Moses to copy?
I've got your attention?
I've got mine.

Everything in the Tabernacle was to be a complete replica of the heavenly. And the only thing God lets Moses decide on the dimensions for was:
The Candlestick.
"Candlestick? What's a candlestick?"
It was the ONE object that allowed all the others to be seen. Without the candlestick it would have been complete darkness. Study the covering of the Tabernacle. There was no natural light getting in, believe me.

The altar. The showbread. The table. All in

darkness without the candlestick. And this is the item God lets Moses choose the dimensions of!
Yes, each part of the tabernacle...
"And you thought it the most boring reading."
Who said that?
(OH IT WAS ME.)

...We thought it the most boring reading but it holds a lifetime of treasures.

The brazen altar, the mercy seat, the outer court, the Holy of Holies, the table of showbread, I could keep us up all night. But the candlestick, which was the only item in the whole of the Tabernacle without dimensions, represented the mind.
All the others...God's mercy, man's devotion, man's service, would have all been lost without the light from the candlestick fed by olive oil which represents the Holy Spirit.
What God was saying is, "Everything has limits. Even the Mercy seat of God. But a human mind illuminated by my Spirit, the Holy Spirit, MY HOLY SPIRIT, has no limits."
Bless the HOLY SPIRIT.
People have said things—against the Father.
People have said things—against the Son.

...But he who says anything against the Holy Spirit shall not be forgiven in this life nor the next.
Matthew 12:32

Yikes! Don't say anything at all against the Godhead. But especially the Holy Spirit, who leads us to Christ and into all truth, who is the earnest of our inheritance, who seals our faith and makes intercession for us when we're speechless, which is more often than not. And that's why blasphemy against the Holy Spirit shall not be forgiven; you're cutting off the Source that leads you to the very Forgiveness you need.

"You seem to study the Old Testament more than the New Testament."

Right now the part of my shirt which should be covering my chest is pulled over my entire face; because...I do.

"You mean you study the Word of God more than the Word of God?"

Yes! The Old Testament is the New concealed.
And the New Testament is the Old revealed.
It's One glorious Book.
And like a fish in the ocean, I'll never see it all.

"Never Jerry! Never! Never!"

That's out of Seinfeld. Kramer is telling Jerry he won't let Little Jerry (his miniature fighting rooster) become a 'never was' because Jerry Seinfeld (the little rooster's name-sake who is concerned about the rooster getting hurt) is now a 'has been.'

"Never Jerry! Never! I won't! I won't! I won't!"

Obviously I don't read all the time. And there is a TV in my house.

Oh, and I do say things against it.

16
AND HE LED THEM TO MARAH

...Because God will never disappoint you.

Hello? The fact of the matter is:

He'll go out of his way to.

Or even better, send you out of your way. You know, to a disappointing situation.

*And he **LED** them to Marah and there they could not drink for the waters were bitter.*
Exodus 15:22,23

1 million human beings in the hot scorching desert longing for water and God Almighty leads them to a place of bitter water: Marah (which means bitter).

"Great, Mommy, we're gonna get to drink. God has led us to water!"

And the people could not drink for the waters were bitter.
Exodus 15:23

"But Mommy, why? Why would God!"

Did most of the mothers have the right answer for their questioning child?
No.

And Israel complained about the bitter waters and chided with Moses.
Exodus 15:24

God led them to bitter waters to expose the bitterness in their lives. He provided the remedy. He always has.

...And Moses cried unto the Lord and the Lord showed him a tree (the cross) *which when he had cast into the waters, the waters* (their lives) *were made sweet.*
Exodus 15:25

When God leads you to a bitter experience in your life it's to expose hidden bitterness and He'll supply the remedy for it. And it's always the Cross.

You think you've suffered. Then consider Christ! What a contradiction of sinners he endured.
Hebrews 12:3

And if you're to follow Me you're to take up your cross and follow Me daily.

Luke 9:23

Sounds like a burden?

But in fact the greatest freedom there is. If we accept bitter experiences as Life's teaching...

"You really bug me sometimes man!" — a midnight student.

"I bug myself!" — the teacher.

P.S. - I didn't just throw out a figure of 1 million human beings being in the scorching desert for effect. **Exodus 12:37** says there were 600,000 men alone, not counting women, children, and adolescent males under 20 at the time. (See **Numbers 1:46,** a year later for that.)

"Thank you. Thank you very much." — Elvis.

17
BURNT STONES
NEHEMIAH

How can I say this? Nehemiah was a cupbearer.

A person whose life was on the line every time the king ate. It was the cupbearer's job to test the wine to make sure it wasn't poisoned.

And after a minute or so if the cupbearer didn't lurch and begin to convulse violently the king knew the wine was okay. "Yea!"

—That was Nehemiah's job.

So...in **Nehemiah 2:1-3**, when the king was on his throne and he noticed Nehemiah sad in his presence no wonder Nehemiah "feared greatly."

Here was a person who died daily, so to speak, whose life was expendable and he was joyless in the king's presence?

"Who gives life to all living things around me!" — And believe me that's what those kings thought.

And that's why Nehemiah feared greatly.

But evidently there was something that the king saw in Nehemiah to the point he appointed him governor of the decimated land of Israel. And let him go on a *short sojourn* to rebuild the city of his fathers.

(Actually the cupbearer in essence became a trusted confidant of the king like someone you'd shoot pool with.)

And once there...
Seeing the hostile environment that the people faced, Nehemiah rebuilt the walls in 52 days and did it all with...

With...

Burnt stones.
Burnt stones?
Yes, burnt stones.

Nebuchadnezzar had burned the city completely at the end of the Israeli nation.

And seeing the distress the people were in and the urgency needed, Nehemiah rebuilt the wall, which would keep the people safe from their enemies, with burnt stones.

Like you and me.
What?
You and me.
God is going to build a great wall for His Church and when He does He's going to do it with burnt stones.

FOR WE ARE A KINGDOM OF LIVING STONES.

God is going to cause a great influx of people into his kingdom and rebuild His wall for his city. And when He does it will be with burnt stones.

People like you and me? And then especially: The unchurched.

People who once went to church but because of circumstances stopped coming.

The unchurched. Burnt stones.

Expect a great influx of burnt stones. God is building the city's wall again. And He will use the once-churched to do it. Those stones that were in the wall. Burned and thrown out of the wall. Now placed again back into the wall.

P.S. — If this is scripture then I should be asking everyone around me to visit my church. Are they a burnt stone?

"I don't know, I haven't asked."

"Me neither."

"But we should."

P.S.S. — Did you notice I italicized *short sojourn*? Nehemiah was governor of Jerusalem from 444 BC to 423 BC. 21 years! He left and basically never came back.

But that's the work of God. We may never return.

18
NOTHING NEW UNDER THE SUN

What would happen...

If we took that literally.
"I do take it literally!"

Or what if we realized there's as much Eternity behind us as there is in front of us?

What has God been doing all this time?
If we live to be eighty years old that's not the equivalent of one thought that crosses our mind in Eternity. God in his mercy won't tell us how old He is.
Or how far in the future He is.
Solomon knew. Kind of.
God inspired him to write the infallible Word of God and he knew...
Kind of.
Just a little.

He wrote in **Ecclesiastes 1:9-12**:

The thing that shall be
Is that that has been
And that that is being done now
Shall be done again
And THERE IS NOTHING NEW UNDER THE SUN (There's that phrase again.)

Is there anything whereof it may be said?
See!
See!
This...
THIS IS NEW! THIS!
No.
IT HAS ALREADY BEEN OF OLD TIME
WHICH WAS BEFORE US
BUT THERE IS NO REMEMBRANCE OF FORMER THINGS
NOR SHALL THERE BE ANY REMEMBRANCE OF THINGS THAT ARE TO COME
WITH THOSE THINGS THAT SHALL EVEN COME AFTER THEM.

What is he saying? That God in His eternity stretching backwards has seen what's on Earth now? Cars. Electricity. Nuclear weapons. Faith.

NOTHING NEW UNDER THE SUN. Has to mean something.

And we thought we took it literally.
But what has God been doing all this time in

Eternity? And there's as much time behind us as there is in front of us. Forever and ever and ever and ever behind us.

We just don't realize it.

What do we think that people like the Apostle Paul and Mother Teresa will be doing? These people gave their entire existence in the service of others for God.

I guarantee you we'll be saying sir and ma'am to some people over there.

> *God is a rewarder of those that diligently seek Him.*
> **Hebrews 11:6**

I can tell you the thief that barely made it on the cross at the time of Christ's crucifixion won't have the influence like a Paul or a Mother Teresa.

But that's…another letter.
Among the ones that are lost.
Yes.
The ones that are missing from this book.
The Lost Letters.

19
WE'RE STILL NOT SATISFIED

"About your exposition on the Solomon and Moses thing."

"We're not."
"No we're not!"
"You never really take us there."

That's been my fault in every chapter.

But do you really want a two-hour lecture? These are **Letters At Midnight**. Not *Lectures*. Thoughts. Crossing a sleepy mind.

But because you insist to know, forgetting that curiosity killed the cat, here it is:

In the time of Moses...God was free.

"What?"

He showed up in a cloud whenever He wanted. And opened the ground and swallowed up His

enemies whenever He wanted too.
Numbers 16:28-34

In Solomon's day, He lived in a temple down the street round the corner up the road. This totally free God who was never catchable in the days of Moses now lived at 1600 King's Avenue, Israel (so to speak).

And for God to say anything against the King in whose land God's house resided was not acceptable. Complaints were not acceptable even "in the name of the Lord."

Read about Jeroboam. God had anointed him king over ten of the twelve tribes of Israel because of Solomon's disobedience. Solomon's!

And what was Solomon's reaction? Was it, "Lord I repent?"

Solomon sought therefore to kill Jeroboam. And Jeroboam fled into Egypt…and was in Egypt until the death of Solomon.
I Kings 11:40

It reminds me of Jesus fleeing as a child into Egypt from the evil King Herod who was trying to kill him. But this isn't King Herod; this is Solomon!

So here's the wisest man on Earth, Solomon, not happy at all with what God had just done. His kingship had co-opted, transcended, become more important of course than the 'rush of God's Spirit.' Those times when God on the spur of the moment just decided to show up and encourage, deliver, rebuke, like in the cloud in Moses' day.

The achievement of Solomon rather consciously or unconsciously served to reverse the dynamic of Moses. And...

Moses would not have been welcome in the court of Solomon. **Chapter 1**.

Yet!
The court had its place.
God in every way intends (obviously when looking at the American church) for His people having rest, leading peaceful productive lives in His Kingdom.

But, why is it that the notion of that peace being threatened with a new thing that God wants to do, that it's then God is met with opposition. Even disobedience.

Why? Because of the fear of change.

We'd rather accept our current livable conditions than to welcome a new move of God. In fact the current consensus, the dominant society, Solomon, will even fight with God because of it.

And the Lord was angry with Solomon, because his heart was turned from the Lord God of Israel, which had appeared unto him twice.

> *Howbeit the Lord would not take the whole kingdom out of his hand: but would keep him a prince all the days of his life for David his servant's sake, whom he chose, because DAVID kept his commandments and his statutes.*
> **I Kings 11:9,34**

It's for the sake of His Son Jesus who became a servant; and to whom He promised, if you endure the cross, I will give you all the nations, tongues and peoples. It's for Jesus' sake God understands our stubbornness. And I use the word 'understands' instead of 'tolerates' on purpose.

"Dude that's harsh!"

You're right. It's Twelve. I was in a hurry and I made the coffee a little strong. It is harsh.

But what God wants is His Kingdom to grow, to become a great kingdom given to His Son, the vine of Adam coming to its fruition. But what He doesn't like is our undying allegiance to Solomon, the dominant culture that He's provided for us to live in.

God tried to correct Solomon's ways through Jeroboam, and Solomon tried to squelch God's voice by killing Jeroboam.

What God would love to see:

Is a grateful people thankful for the years of peace and prosperity He's given us.

Passionate for the lifestyle He commands humans to live.

Even if now in opposition to our comfortable

settled "*I've got to take the kids to soccer*" lives, it costs us everything. Everything.

"Why not just leave Jeroboam in Egypt and us up here?"

"Why didn't Solomon go after him? Jeroboam was gone in another country."

Because being the wisest man, he knew if it's God's will, Jeroboam will show back up!

"It's too late for this."

"Isn't it midnight?"

"Who holds a class this late anyway? Good grief."

It is *good grief*. And one we must experience if we are to grow.

20
HEART OF JERUSALEM

Our leaders had a meeting in Jerusalem late last night.
Israel's elite in festive array, yeah it was quite a sight.
Caiaphas with hands held high toasting a wealthy crowd.
When a solider rides up, he tilts his head with his cup
　Exchanges whispers then laughs out loud.
They've learned of an olive garden where the Nazarene often goes.
It's there they'll finally nab him, in fact tonight, when nobody knows.
And they thanked their lucky stars as the world's elite fell in a trance
Thinking of the glory of this man! While waiting their chance
In the Heart of Jerusalem.
Man Jesus is something he does everything just right.
The mute when healed shout, "Hallelujah!" as he gives a blind beggar sight.
A funeral procession he turned into a party in the alley.
A little girl who suddenly died he suddenly returned back to her daddy.

And then He'll stop as the crowd rushes by.
We'll think, "Lord what do you see?" — as He stares at the clear blue sky.
"You'll long to see just one more day of the Son of Man."
Then shrug His shoulders and say, "I smell trouble brewing in the Heart of Jerusalem."
In the emerald halls of Heaven a proud Father sings his Son's praise.
Angels dancing in the golden streets to the song the choir plays.
Below in Hell's dungeons Satan's nameless minions tremble to a brand new song.
On Earth, in a smoke filled tavern, a lonely instrument plays...till dawn.
Outside the city morning breaks.
On a hill shaped like a skull with wooden crosses popping out its head
In the chilling morning air a man, naked, shivering, shakes
The best person to ever live so loving so caring so tender.
Healing this time man's sin — requires a bloody touch
From hands viciously nailed to a timber.
In the City Uptown, not a solitary sound, angels stand silent in the street.
A helpless Father looks away, pushes the moon in front of the sun, turns out the light.
But then below, Hell catches fire in a brand new blaze!

As Death, Hell and the Grave collapse on their knees.
There's a fourth man in the fire untouched by the
 flames!
With nail pierced hands demanding the keys.
Then he steps over the chasm, into Abraham's
 bosom.
Preaches to the faithful in Paradise the Good News
As one arm of His Cross stretches back in time.
And the other arm, His Gospel sent to the living, to all
 the generations to come!
Of His death, burial
AND RESURRECTION
His great work he accomplished
In the Heart of Jerusalem
In the Heart of Jerusalem.

Performed at Advent 2005

21
DÉJÀ VU

"Hello I'm back, tonight...
"Yes tonight! If it's possible—
"I'd like to impart a piece of the divine."

Even as God does in the night.
The Psalms teach us that God gives unto His beloved *while* they sleep.

> *For He gives to His beloved even in their sleep.*
> **Psalm 127:2** (NAS)

Now you know what déjà vu is.
"Déjà vu is a mystery none can fathom!"
The great God who says again in Scripture:

He goes before you to prepare you a place.
Then follows after you as your rear guard.
Isaiah 58:8

In those times what you call déjà vu is actually God saying: *I told you you'd be here. One night long ago. In a dream you didn't remember.*

Webster's defines déjà vu as: The illusion or feeling of having already experienced something actually being experienced for the first time. It's French for, "already seen."
Already seen? Like a dream.
But when it comes to pass we think, "Wow I've been here before."

Sleep therapists say we dream on the average five dreams a night.
"Man I haven't journaled all of mine."
Déjà vu is God saying, *I AM with you*.
You may experience déjà vu in a good time.
A bad time.
In whatever time the Father sees fit.

To let you know right then, right there, "I AM WITH YOU. I told you you'd be *here*."

AT THAT EXACT MOMENT! YOU'D BE THERE.

"...And no one can take this experience of déjà vu away from you because it's yours and yours alone."
Through the happy times or bad.

Always.

Till the end of the Age.

Amen.

22
081689

Wow! What was that about?

I'm remembering a dream I had back in the late 80's. That day I had walked out of the Spirit as much as any person could. Heaven help the angel that'd have crossed my path. (Actually Heaven help me.)

So how in the world could I go to prayer that night. You see I was in a prayer group that met every Tuesday. We'd take all the prayer requests from the previous Sunday, a monstrous stack of cards, (Monstrous?—We were coming against the works of the devil) and pray over each individual one. It was a ministry that rivaled the missionary journeys of Paul. Well...praying for your particular body of believers cannot be over stressed.

Anyway how could I go? But I said, "Lord I'm going. I repent for today. And I know you still expect me to fulfill my obligation of praying for your local body."

You do know that Zacharias, the father of John the Baptist, when fulfilling his duty in the temple had the audacity to argue with an angel (most assuredly Gabriel) and was struck dumb for it.

So I went! I prayed. Felt wonderful. Went home.
To bed. Had a dream.

081689
On the road called Harding Place, the road I took every day to work; a long line of pedestrians just standing had formed and every one was waiting to go through the checkpoint at the top of the road where it intersected. You could break in line; no one cared. You went your own pace.

I broke all the way to the front and as I was walking through the front entrance Jesus! stopped me. Very ashamed I looked down.

He touched my arm and said, "All ships get blown off their courses. The important thing is, you got back on yours."

I said, "yes sir," and went in.

Inside was a banquet hall and we sat down waiting for the festivities to begin. I then noticed that the silverware didn't match. I thought, "the silverware doesn't match, it doesn't even match."

Then the Spirit softly, calmly, spoke to me and said, "It's His treasure from the sea. He loves diversity."

"Oh! Of course." —I obviously

```
didn't belong there.
```

But was summoned anyway.
The book of Revelations likens the sea to peoples, multitudes and nations.

Revelation 17:15

And God has treasure from that sea.

Thou art worthy...for thou hast redeemed us, out of every kindred, tongue, people, and nation.

Revelation 5:9

Yes, you and me.

23
LECTURES AT MIDNIGHT

"Actually I think the Word of God is like a rock, and I haven't even scratched the surface yet." (Chapter 11)

"So speak to it! The way Moses spoke to the Rock in the Wilderness and let it gush out its Life Giving Waters to you."

> *For they were all baptized unto Moses in the cloud and in the sea. And did all eat the same spiritual meat; and did all drink the same spiritual drink: for they drank of that spiritual Rock that followed them; and that Rock was Christ.*
> **I Corinthians 10:2-4**

"What Rock, what are you talking about?"

(I'm rubbing my eyes right now only because it's midnight and not because I'm a frustrated teacher wearied by his students.)

"What teacher holds a class this late anyway!"

Who threw that?!

The nation of Israel was in the desert for forty

years. A place where there is no water. And having a populace numbering in the hundreds of thousands, the daily water consumption must have been staggering. How in the world did God accomplish that?

We know how He fed them. Everyday with manna—angel's bread they gathered each morning.

We know how he shielded them from the desert extremes: With a cloud by day to block the scorching heat and a pillar of fire at night to keep them from the desert's chill.

We know how not a single person went into the desert sick; for the night of the Passover, God miraculously touched every person who needed healing to make their Exodus easier. We know their clothes and shoes didn't wear out.

But how in the world did God supply the rivers of water needed to sustain a nation in a place void of all natural moisture? How?

By a Rock. A boulder the Israelites carried with them wherever they journeyed.

It was the Rock God had told Moses to smite the very first time there arose a need for water. It's at the same time when God instituted the daily provision of manna from Heaven. At the very beginning!

Exodus 16 & 17

(How is it we know about the manna and not about the Rock.)

And the people thirsted there for water and

> *the people murmured against Moses, and said, why is it that you have brought us up out of Egypt to kill us and our children and our cattle with thirst!*
>
> *And Moses cried unto the Lord saying, what shall I do unto this people? They be almost ready to stone me.*
>
> *And the Lord said unto Moses. Go on before the people and take with thee of the elders of Israel and thy rod wherewith thou smotest the river, take in thine hand and go.*
>
> *Behold I will stand before thee there upon the rock in Horeb and thou shalt smite the rock and there shall come water out of it, that the people may drink.*
>
> *And Moses did so in the sight of the elders of Israel.*
>
> *And he called the name of the place Massah and Meribah, because of the chiding of the children of Israel and because they tempted the lord saying:*
>
> *"Is the Lord among us or not?"*

Exodus 17:3-7

That Rock never left.
They never abandoned it.
And it was so important it even kept Moses from entering the Promised Land.

> *And the people abode in Kadesh...and there was no water for the congregation and they*

> *gathered against Moses and Aaron.*
>
> *And they spoke saying, "would to God He'd have killed us when our brethren died before the Lord!"*

(This is in **Numbers 20**. One and a half books of the Bible later and years after the first occurrence with the Rock. These people had been living every day for decades in the miraculous. Their shoes, their clothes, their health, the manna, the cloud, the pillar of fire; how could they be that angry with God? Why? Because every single thing was provided automatic for them except the water, and *they resented* having to ask God for it.)

> *And Moses and Aaron went from the presence of the assembly unto the door of the tabernacle of the congregation, and they fell upon their faces: and the glory of the Lord appeared unto them.*
>
> *And the Lord spake unto Moses, saying,*
>
> *Take the rod, and gather thou the assembly together, thou and Aaron thy brother and speak ye unto the rock before their eyes, and it shall give forth his water and thou shalt bring forth to them water out of the rock: so thou shalt give the congregation and their beasts drink.*
>
> *And Moses took the rod from before the Lord as He commanded him.* (This is huge people, huge.)
>
> *And Moses gathered the congregation*

together before the rock and said to them, "Hear now you rebels, must we fetch you water out of this rock."

(You see, daily they gathered their food for themselves and their families; and daily they were to speak to the rock for their water also.)

And Moses lifted up his hand and with his rod he smote the rock twice.

Moses struck it once. Nothing happened.
Moses you're supposed to be speaking to the rock. And he struck it twice and it gave forth its water.

And the Lord spake unto Moses and Aaron, because ye believed Me not, to sanctify Me in the eyes of the children of Israel, therefore ye shall not bring this congregation into the land which I have given them.
Numbers 20:12

Moreover, brethren, I would not have you ignorant, how that all our fathers were under the cloud, and all passed through the sea…and all did drink the same spiritual drink:
*For THEY DRANK OF THAT SPIRITUAL ROCK THAT FOLLOWED THEM: **AND THAT ROCK WAS CHRIST**.*
I Corinthians 10:1-4

Moses was one of the most important people (if not the most important person) in the whole of the Old Testament. He's the only person God ever buried.
Deuteronomy 34:5,6

And he wasn't allowed to lead the people into the Promised Land because he smote that Rock, when he was told to speak to it.

P.S. — God told Moses to speak to the Rock but *commanded* Moses in **Numbers 20 verse 8** to take the rod with him also. *Specifically commanded Moses to take the rod to that meeting!*

Did God give him an opportunity to fail when addressing the hostile crowd?
And why the Tree of Knowledge in the Garden of Eden? Why even put it there if partaking of it's evil.
And! —If Moses was set up to fail, did he have a problem with that? He seemed pretty content at the Mt. of Transfiguration in the New Testament 1,400 years later dressed in just-less-than Jesus' blazing white.

But all shall be answered!
Just not in this book.
And certainly not by me.

Though we will discuss Moses again...in other...**Letters At Midnight**.

24
"YEAH MOSES!"
(WITH CLINCHED FISTS)

"Would you please expound the teaching on the Solomonic Moment vs. the Moses Dynamic?"

I have many things that I would say unto you, but you cannot bear them now.
John 16:12

- Jesus often says this to me.

The Solomonic moment: The Golden Age of Israel. A time of unrivaled prosperity. When God had given Israel peace on all sides and the individual could enjoy the works of their hands unhindered by cares and under the shade of their own 'fig tree.'

1) Unrivaled prosperity.
2) Peace on all sides.
3) Unhindered individual goals.

The American church has enjoyed all of these for

many years. The Golden Age of Israel has been the experience of The American Church.

But alas! (—only a word Jeremiah bewails in the book of **Lamentations** when his culture has collapsed, completely.) Yes alas! the Solomonic moment, which we as Christians have enjoyed, is ending. The dominant culture in which the American church resides is turning hostile towards our way of thinking and lifestyle.

We can do two things. Deny our faith and change our lifestyle to fit the culture in which we live or we can become the Moses dynamic and be God's grace and power to a dying, hurting society whose Managers are outwardly critical towards us.

"But why? If this is true why would God be allowing the American Church, the world's number one missionary provider, to go through this?"

"Yeah why?"

"Why!"

Perhaps a study of the American church: we find that it is so enculturated by society to the point where the moors of the day takes precedence over our faith.

And going one step farther, Jesus said in **John 9:4**

For the night cometh when no man can work.

Like in the days of the Caesars of Rome, or in the days of the Soviet Union, and even now in China. And it will get to the point in the U.S. that to be passionate about our faith even in the Spirit of Love, will be considered as hate language. Christ's teachings were considered in every above-mentioned example as ultimately hate language; a critical opinion against the then Dominant Culture. Do we think our society, who's turning from Christian ideals will be any different towards us?

THE NIGHT COMETH WHEN NO MAN CAN WORK.

Jesus was speaking about sharing our faith.

And famous modern day statesmen, when in the presence of a holy God, are going to be shocked. They will be speechless.
Did not Jesus say, many will come to me in that day and say Lord, Lord did we not confess we knew you...and He'll say, *but you didn't; your lifestyle proved that.*

Every single age thinks it's the most modern, the most up-to-date, the one with the most Light. But the Word of God doesn't change. Societies do, they come and go.

"Just because you're an American doesn't mean you're a Christian."
I remember hearing my pastor say that for the first time. I assumed it did. Or at least assumed being an American living in a Christian culture gave you a

better chance of being one. But as this culture digresses towards darkness being automatically a Christian American won't even be an issue, will it?

So as the days progress when the church is moved from the Solomonic moment and it is no longer at peace with the culture with which it cohabits and finds itself in the midst of a hostile dominant culture with which it is at odds:

Moses will show up.

Judgments will happen. Ouch!

The word 'judgment' is not politically correct now remember:

"All is relevant."

"Everyone's individual experience is valid."

"What is truth?" Pilate asked. (A Manager of the dominant culture.)

"I am the Way, the Truth, and the Life," Jesus proclaimed. (A marginal one.)

And the Egyptians were all drowned on the seashore.

Exodus 14:30

(God's last say.)

But let's reach out before God has His last say.

For He is not willing that any should perish but that all come unto repentance.

"Are you saying head God's judgment off by His mercy?"

Why...He may sling another galaxy into existence if we did that.

25
LETTERS AT MIDNIGHT

The sum of the matter is this: After the attack of 9/11 this Nation will never be the same. This nation who ruled with open borders and the motto, "Who Would Dare."

Weeks after the attack of 9/11 I saw in a vision two animals locked in mortal combat; and the wind was blowing the fiercest I'd ever seen it. It was the middle of the night and so dark.

"Was it déjà vu?"

Please don't interrupt. We are treading into perilous times. The greatest nation on earth is being challenged externally and internally. Our mores are changing while the world is questioning our validity also.

Here we, in our darkest hour, are asking ourselves, 'who are we?'

While the world is saying, "enough of America."

It's high time we as God's people crawl on our knees.

Oh! This saying gloriously offends me.

Let's park our Lexuses and beg God for His mercy. We fight an enemy unseen, in the Heavenlies!

Nostradamus wrote the attack on New York would mark a 26-year war. Others say the oceans will rise until the coastlands are lost to water. God says the Earth will be destroyed by fire.

"Which is it?"

"All could come true, in succession."

People are crying *it's the end of the world* and there's been some extraordinary generations that have cried this. At the time of the Great Death, The Black Plague, which decimated Europe and killed untold millions; read the despairing literature of that day. All knew the world was ending.

Or more recent history: WWI. And then especially WWII, when certainly an Antichrist stood on the world's scene.

When peoples of the pacific islands or the tropics have seen their lives destroyed by floods, earthquakes, or famines. All have believed the end of the world was at hand.

And all these generations of people through the centuries that have cried *the end of the world!* All have one thing in common. They were wrong. It wasn't the end of the world.

And what if it's not *the end of the world* now? You and I have to be prepared for that. Not The End Of The World.

ISN'T IT CURIOUS.

We tell the lost to be prepared for the end of the world; but we as Christians must be prepared if it's

NOT.

Where will we be in culture? Where does that leave us?

One of the most common fallacies when interpreting biblical prophecy is to filter it through our contemporary grid of familiarities. For example, when Hal Lindsay wrote of the millions of locusts in Revelations coming from the bottomless pit to torment mankind, after reading of their characteristics he mused if it couldn't be talking about the US Cobra helicopters. Don't laugh, it makes for great reading, sold millions of books and I've got to say, if the US had to build that many helicopters there'd be enormous military contracts awarded and the growing jobless American public could all go back to work. But who wants to build helicopters to make war with.

Still, I worry about the jobless American public.

What will they eat?

What about their bills to pay?

John the Baptist ate wild honey and locusts. But you'd break a tooth biting this new metal kind of locust, huh.

But did you also know there's a plant native to that area of the world which is called the Locust plant. Insect or foliage, it doesn't matter what he really ate. He came calling for repentance. And that's what we need to do. What I need to do. Repent and pray for this Nation. A Nation whose foundation was the Christian Ethos; and whether all were believers or not, those Christian valves of our culture kept us in safe waters instead of the social tsunami that is surely coming.

We saw in **Ezekiel**...

"What, the Old Testament again?"

You're the one who made the crack about déjà vu aren't you. Okay, but when will we embrace that the New Testament is primarily concerned with the spiritual and physical health of the individual; and the Old Testament is primarily concerned with the spiritual and physical health of Culture. Both are monumental to God.

So we saw in **Ezekiel** that at the end of the Jewish State that God sent and destroyed his own dwelling place. And in the book of **Jeremiah** it tells how God left the prophet there so Jeremiah could experience first hand and record his thoughts and feelings and weep (and write the book of **Lamentations**) for the people who should have been grieving over the death and decay of their land, but who had been fooled until the total destruction of *everyone's* dwelling place.

—While the Managers of the Dominant Society kept saying, "everything is fine, in fact, finally things are the way things should have always been. There is finally true freedom for all. For all. How dare you speak of Christian absolutes."

Listen to Jeremiah's simple response to that mindset.

> *Thus saith the Lord of Host, the God of Israel. Amend your ways and your doings, and I will cause you to dwell in this place. Trust you not in lying words, saying, The temple of the Lord!* (We are a Christian culture) *The temple of the Lord!* (Although it doesn't seem as much of a Christian culture) *The temple of the Lord!* (Then what will it be like when we are not a Christian culture?) *are these.*
>
> **Jeremiah 7:3-4**

Now read the rest of the chapter and it is a mirror of modern day society. And God assures us, like in the days of Jeremiah, we will not continue dwelling in this place—the peace, freedom, rest, affluence, safety, etc. that we have been used to.

But enough. It's late. Does it seem late to you?

> *For the night is far spent and the day is at hand.*
>
> **Romans 13:12**

What day is he speaking of? The day when we reap what we have sown?

> *Therefore let us wake to righteousness and the day star rise in our hearts.*

And walking from his computer, he hit the table and spilled the *cold coffee*. I told you it was late.

What?! I can't italicize my words only His?

26
TWO KINDS OF PEOPLE

There are two kinds of people in the world.

Those who are conforming the Image of God to themselves, and those who are being conformed into the Image of God.

Some years ago archeologists did a study on South American Cultures. These primitive peoples at the center of their life had totems.

(Primitive peoples? If the Lord tarries people in the year 3,000 will think we were still dragging our knuckles.) Anyway! These primitive peoples had visible images of the gods they worshipped. Curiously each totem reflected the traits that each particular tribe saw themselves as possessing.

For example: The tribe that saw itself as very stealthy and secretive, its totem's head was a crocodile. And the one that saw itself separate from the others in power and attacking ability, its totem was usually a great cat indigenous to that area.

You see?

Every time the worshiper bowed down to worship their god, the totem, what they were actually worshipping was the image of themselves.

And then...

There's us. Those who are being conformed into the image of Christ.

Yes! Us...who constantly repent.

Who say, "Lord please forgive me, I see your standard. Perfection. Know who you are. Want to be just like you. Find myself not. Realize your mercy. Experience your love."

Repent. "Yes Lord I repent. Change me and I will be changed."

And that's all it takes. Scriptures teach that God subjected all creation unto vanity.

"He knew we'd fail?"

"Glorious!"

—We've always known it and now God does!

—At least we now realize God does.

The group that is blessed by God is the one that says, "Lord, I won't make a totem and change You to fit my image and the lifestyle approved by the culture in which I live. I'll repent, confessing it's your image I want to mirror, not mine or my culture's."

Amen. And amen.

27
I DON'T LIKE THE CURRENT PRESIDENT

Well...

Remember when Daniel set his heart to pray and intercede for his people? Remember? **Daniel 10**.

It says on the first day of his three-week fast that his prayer was heard and a *certain* angel was sent, yet who was detained the whole time by the Prince of Persia. Remember that in **Chapter 10** of the book of **Daniel**.

Guess who was the world power at the time. Persia. And Scripture says the Prince of Persia stood up against him. The Prince of Persia. (The Main Fallen Angel of the World's Main Super Power at the time.)

In the whole of Scripture, Old Testament and New, there's only two angels mentioned by name: Michael and Gabriel. And one of these was detained by the angel that governed the most powerful kingdom of the world at that time.

Gabriel – the Messenger telling of The Greatest

Things God's Going To Do.
Michael – the Angel of War.

What is God telling us?
If I'm a Mover-and-a-Shaker, I won't bother with the homeless.

"Huh!"
"What!"

The most powerful evil angel that governed the most powerful world kingdom at the time himself stood in opposition to divine help. To Gabriel.
And here we are saying we don't like our current President who leads the undisputed most powerful nation on Earth.
So most assuredly the powers against us in the heavens are congregated over America.
Let us pray daily for him. Whether Clinton, Bush, Obama, Democratic, Republican, whoever! Let us pray.

God lead our President. Open the eyes of his understanding. Keep him from evil influences. Bless him, Lord, that we may lead peaceful, godly lives in your sight. Lord, we ask You to bless the President You've given us. Bless him, Lord, with wisdom and clarity to do what is right in your sight, O God.

Amen and amen.

28
THE LORD IS GOD OF THE HILLS BUT HE IS NOT GOD OF THE VALLEYS

When God nitpicks...Oh glorious.

He loves us; it's always for our good. When God nitpicks, He's gonna do great things, yes sir.

In the Old Testament (before the New when the glorious Son of God washed us clean by his own blood) when the children of Israel had nothing going for them, nothing good that God could look on; when they were in dire straits with their enemies, it was then He found fault. He nitpicked, *with their enemies* not them.

Israel was in total rebellion yet, God, who grieved at seeing the distress his people were in, found (sought) a reason to help his disobedient children.

He nitpicked:

The enemies of Israel said in **I Kings 20:28**.

> *And there came a man of God, and spake unto the king of Israel, and said, Thus saith the Lord, because the Syrians have said, The Lord is God of the hills, but he is not God of the valleys, therefore will I deliver all this great multitude into thine hand, and ye shall know that I am the Lord.*

Just because they think God is only over the mountains, not the valleys, He's going to deliver his people from a great gigantic enemy? There's a world of worse opinions of God out there. And here God is responding to this one. This small one.

Who was the king of Israel at this time? Ahab. Hello! Ahab. Undoubtedly one of the worst recorded kings of Israel. And if you continue reading the story, even after God delivers their enemies into their hands, immediately Ahab disobeys when seeing he's safe again.

But...

Yet...

When God the Father had absolutely no reason to help his rebellious children, He went out of His way to find a reason. He nitpicked.

Is God nitpicking in your life?

Be thankful He is.

Things are looking up then.

Praise God.
Blessed are those He chastens. More nitpicking?
"Trust me," says the Lord. "I am God of your valleys."

29
MOSES
&
THE PROMISED LAND

My mother was taught that Moses died lost because he was not allowed to cross over into the Promised Land because of his disobedience when striking the rock. And everyone knows the Promised Land represents Heaven.

...Oh please.
Yikes. Oh please.
It merely would have broken God's symbolism. And God's into symbols:

THE LAMB OF GOD.
THE TREE OF LIFE.
RIVERS OF LIVING WATER.
BREAD OF LIFE.
GOOD SHEPHERD.
LION OF THE TRIBE OF JUDAH.
BRIGHT AND MORNING STAR.

Need I say more. Moses was the lawgiver and he was about to cross over into the Promised Land.

"No Moses, the Law can't get you into the promises of God, only Grace. The Law is a schoolteacher bringing us to Christ. Bringing us to the Promised Land. Where all the promises of God are yes in Christ Jesus.

"And no I won't tell you your color, so quit asking." —That's out of the movie *The Village* where the blind heroine must cross miles of uncharted woods to get "medicines from the towns" to save the man she loves. It was her burden and hers alone.

So no! I won't site every scriptural reference; look it up yourself. But I digress.

When the Israelites crossed the Jordan to go into the Promised Land, it wasn't symbolizing the individual's physical death and going to Heaven. But what it symbolized was the one way God's people, all of God's people, are to enter the Promised Land

Being born of his Spirit. The River of Living Water.

For under the law all die (SO MOSES HAD TO DIE!); but under grace all are made alive.

"Besides you're 126 years old, do you really want to continue carrying this complaining people?"

"Lord you're right, just let me see your glory. Let me see your glory."

And he did.

Mt. of Transfiguration...Elijah and Moses appeared talking with our Lord.

The Promise Land of Canaan had giants and problems and provision, grapes the size of tennis balls. The Christian walk has problems.

In this world you shall have tribulation.

And the Lord will prepare you a table in the midst of your enemies.

O my what a glorious God we serve.

Moses was the lawgiver and the law cannot get you into the Promises of God. Only Grace. By Joshua the Son of Nun. A type of the Christ of course.

P.S. You do know the first one to break the Law of God was the lawgiver. Literally:

And when Moses saw that the people were naked (for Aaron had made them naked unto their shame among their enemies)...*that it came to pass as soon as Moses came nigh unto the camp* (from Mt. Sinai after forty days of fasting like Jesus in the wilderness) *that he saw the calf, and the dancing, and Moses' anger waxed hot, and he cast the tables out of his hands* (written by the finger of God no less) *and brake them beneath the mount.*

Exodus 32:25 & 19

God's giving us a picture here. Not even the lawgiver was good enough. Who acted in God's Righteous anger! But we all need Grace, the unmerited mercy of God.

So live by Grace. And experience the promises of God in your life.

Hey, these are **Letters at Midnight**, I'm tired.

"I don't appreciate you writing letters at midnight. It exposes too much light into my secret places."

Letters at Midnight exposing light. You do of course see the irony here?

Creeping up to deepest darkest time of night...light shines on the dark places of the human heart.

And Jesus arose a great while before day and began to pray.

And he flipped the switch and the coffee began to perk.

—Well...what did you expect...Man! My writing's not as good as His. But oh well.

30
THE LAST SUPPER

The upper room was furnished
There was bread and wine to drink
Jesus' words became so poignant
None of us wanted to think

My heart started beating harder
As he said he was going away
We all thought, "Lord where will you go?"
But none of us had a thing to say

And the Son of God who spoke
The worlds into being could tell
No matter what he said this time
With God going away
Human countenance fell

...He gave a couple reasons
Saying one day we'd all see
Then told a story of a good Shepherd
Who lost his life for his sheep

We knew exactly what he was saying
John leaned over to get close

All of us just stared into the distance
Thomas' eyes were closed

And the Son of God
Who spoke the worlds into being could tell
No matter what He said this time
With God going away
Human countenance fell

Human countenance fell
Human countenance fell.

31
NERO KESRON

Caesar Nero Kesron
Tell me how can this be?
Rome's legions with swords held high
All lie dead in glory

And driving to church tonight
It becomes clear to see
The Kingdom you sought to destroy
Remains while you're history

    Well I guess, time did tell, those you killed, gave the Victory Yell

Caesar Nero Kesron
Oh the world may never know
The glory that was Greece
The grandeur that was Rome

For your ancient Colosseum
Monument of Tyranny
Tourist walk the cobble stones
Children yell, "Mommy see!"

Well I guess, time did tell, those you killed, gave the
    Victory Yell
Yes I guess, time did tell, those you killed, gave the
    Victory Yell

Hey you with the numbered name
Caesar Kesron Nero
The Revelation is people like you
All add up to zero

God still sends the proud away
Even if it takes a thousand years
We laugh till water fills our eyes
And God wipes away our tears

Well I guess, time did tell, those you killed, gave the
    Victory Yell.
Well I guess, time did tell, those you killed, gave the
    Victory Yell.

32

THE DOMINANT CULTURE

Still not satisfied?!

"We are satisfied."

Okay then. —The only way we will change our society for good is to realize that it's insane.

"What?"

Insane like Jesus did. When on the cross He cried:

Father forgive them, for they know not what they do!
Luke 23:34

Jesus is asking His Father to forgive the dominant culture for killing Him because they're insane and don't know what they're doing.

What did you think, *"They don't know what they do!"* meant?

The world was insane by crucifying the Son of God who'd made them and who'd come to help them.

Jesus was pleading for mercy for this society by reason of its insanity.

Mercy by reason of insanity? Which is often

sought in modern society, ask any State supreme court.

So where does that leave us? Well...
Here's Jesus, the one being killed by the insane person, asking mercy for that same insane person. Therefore:

When considering your own circumstances...

Consider Him who endured such a contradiction of sinners.
Hebrews 12:3

He certainly expects us to at least tell them there's a kingdom of God, which is all about:

*POWER, AND LOVE, AND OF A **SOUND MIND**.*
I Timothy 1:7

"I'm quitting class."
"I never was even *in* this class."
"You ask too much."
"You actually expect us to be the light of the world!"
Who am I talking to? You people who have overcome the evil one.
I John 2:13

"A bruised reed in which the Son of God in His care won't damage worse."

Isaiah 42:3

Turn? - And here we are giving in to the modern consensus: 'live like you want,' 'every lifestyle is relevant,' and 'far be it from me to tell you what is right.'

> *For the priest's lips should keep knowledge, and they should seek the law at his mouth: for he is the messenger of the lord of hosts.*
Malachi 2:7

> *...And has made us a kingdom of priests unto his God.*
Book of Revelation

Yes I'm doing this all from memory; it's after midnight and I'm on a roll.

We're the salt of the earth; don't be judgmental but be the truth!

What we should be saying is, "big deal so you're in bondage to....By the power of Jesus you're now delivered!"

We can't offer that power if we're not in opposition to the lifestyle. And the one thing that will penetrate the lifestyle is...

Is...

Is...

Compassion.

Scriptures speak over and over again that Jesus,

when feeling compassion, healed them. It's one thing being critical of the lost's lifestyle; it's another thing all together, energizing the person with delivering compassion that draws them from the destructive lifestyle they're in.

Moses was from the ultimate fringe of society.
We're supposed to reach those untouchable by most humans.
For remember: And Moses drove his cattle farther out than anyone.
He came to offer justice and mercy.
Saying that God sees you:

The overlooked.
The marginal.
The thrown-away.
The leftover.

God sees you. And has come to help.

33
EVANGELISM EXPLOSION

Years ago I was in an outreach called Evangelism Explosion. A ministry started by a Church of Christ guy.

"Church of Christ?"

Yeah, and I was Pentecostal roots.

"Boy there's two different tribes of Israel."

"One congregation completely a cappella and the other with trumpets blaring, swinging from chandeliers."

DENOMINATIONS, DENOMINATIONS, GET YOUR DENOMINATIONS!

"Charlie Brown isn't it great?"

And one of the many things I got out of it was he told an analogy saying:

"What if one of the people you lived with daily committed only three sins a day. Just three sins. And even these were in thought only. Imagine a person perfect in actions, perfect in words, and only in thought sinning three times a day. To the people around that person they would seem like the most perfect saint."

"He never says anything unkind."
"She never does anything wrong!"

But still they sin in thought three times a day. 3 times 365 days is approximately 1,000 sins a year. If the person lived to be 70, that's 70,000+ sins.
70,000 crimes against the holiness of God.
The most perfect person we'd ever met was in fact a habitual criminal—he or she committing crimes three times every single day of their life.
"What a horrible person."

You can see why the high Priest rushed in once a year with innocent blood, sprinkled it on the Mercy Seat, and then fled quickly.
The lost don't know how lost they are.
And we don't know how saved we are.
And how we should share the loving gospel.
The loving gospel.

Come now and let us reason together, saith the Lord; though your sins be as scarlet, they shall be as white as snow; though they be red like crimson, they shall be as wool.

As far as the east is from the west, so far has He removed our transgressions from us.

The lost don't know how lost they are. And we, the found, how found we are.

But you are a chosen generation, a royal priesthood, a holy nation, a special race.

"But no one will be interested in the Treasure in me," we think.

And then there are those Christians who because of life's circumstances even feel:

I have loved you saith the Lord. Yet you say, wherein hast thou loved us?
Malachi 1:2

May we never go there. But right now I have a finger pointing at you.

And that means...I have THREE pointing back at me.

The Father, the Son and the Holy Spirit.

Letters At Midnight.

We wouldn't have wanted them to be easy.

THE END

Yes the End. No I won't change the ending. Abrupt endings are life.

And how many loved ones we knew whose life ended...

AND WE SHALL ALL STAND IN OUR PLACE. THE PLACE WHERE WE'LL BE THE MOST HAPPIEST! AT THE END OF OUR DAYS.
(THE BOOK OF DANIEL)

...Okay I repent. You win. Decades ago there was this huge Baptist Church in Arkansas and one Sunday on a pew way down front, among a thousand church goers, a little boy kept picking at his little sister, all dressed up in her nice Sunday dress. The boy's father (this really happened) kept warning the lad that if he didn't stop he'd be taken out and spanked. The child kept it up when finally the dad grabbed the child's arm and said, 'let's go.' The boy suddenly realizing the gravity of his situation and beginning the trek up the long church aisle with hundreds of people looking yelled, "Somebody pray!"

"Now the End has come. And I face the final curtain." —**Elvis.**

www.ingramcontent.com/pod-product-compliance
Lightning Source LLC
Chambersburg PA
CBHW021410290426
44108CB00010B/461